How We Grow

Florence Condidorio

Copyright © 2023 Florence Condidorio
All rights reserved
First Edition

PAGE PUBLISHING
Conneaut Lake, PA

First originally published by Page Publishing 2023

ISBN 979-8-88960-371-9 (pbk)
ISBN 979-8-88960-391-7 (digital)

Printed in the United States of America

Contents

Chapter 1 1

Chapter 2 3

Chapter 3 6

Chapter 4 10

Chapter 5 15

Chapter 6 19

Chapter 7 46

Chapter 8 55

Chapter 9 67

Chapter 10 78

A Dream, a Vision, a Reality, a Sensory Park 85

Chapter 1

This is the beginning. My memories begin as a five-year-old child, who came down with polio.

We were at my grandfather and grandmother's house in Canada, visiting my mother's family. We were there to help my grandfather as my grandma was ill. One morning, I woke up and was feeling sick. I got up and started to walk; after a few steps, I fell down. I got up again and started to walk again and took two or three steps and fell down again. After two or three days, I was still walking and falling down after a few steps. My grandfather and my mother became very concerned and took me to the doctors. They explained the situation to the doctor. He examined me and said that I was putting on and that I was looking for attention. After that, I got a lot of attention from all my aunts and uncles living at the house, but I continued walking and falling down after a couple of steps. After some time, my grandfather and mother decided that they needed to take me to see a different doctor. We went to see the second doctor. They explained to the doctor what the problem was and what the other doctor had said. The doctor said to me, "Little girl, walk across the room." I remember that part vividly. Of course, I did that, and after a couple of steps, I would fall and get up and start walking and fall again. The doctor told them I had polio and that the family would have to be under quarantine. He also told them they would have to take me to the hospital so I could be taken care of there. Of course, I did not understand all of what was being said or understand what was happening. At the hospital, they put a cast on me from my toes to the hip. After that, I couldn't remember much of anything, returning to my grandparents' house or how we returned to the States, as my parents didn't have a car at that time. Unfortunately, over the years, I forgot to ask my mother about some of the questions that I had.

Chapter 2

I will share with you the memories I have now of what went on after our return home.

For a while, our family stayed in our home as we were all quarantined. Next, I remember sitting on our porch at home, in a chair, with my casted leg elevated. Many relatives and neighbors came over and sat and talked with me. Next, I remember being told that I had to go away to a hospital to learn how to walk again. My father was Genesee County's first deputy sheriff. I give you this information because the sheriff's car pulled up in front of my house one morning. My father carried me out in his arms to the sheriff's car and placed me in it. I remember my mother at the front door crying. I was transported in the sheriff's car to the Ithaca Hospital as my parents still did not have a car.

I remember when we got to the hospital, the nurse put me in a large crib, and my father kissed me goodbye and left. I cried, and the nurses tried to console me. We had supper and then went to bed. I lived there for six months. I remember feeling very sad and crying a lot. Several times, when my parents were able to borrow a car, they did come to visit me. I remember feeling so happy to see them. I do remember playing with two little boys named Jimmy and Raymond.

I was a bed wetter. One night, one of the nurses was very upset with me because of the bed-wetting. She threatened me, if I wet the bed one more time, she would put a diaper on me and show me to all the adults in the hospital with the diaper on. I can remember being afraid. This did cure my bed-wetting. I do remember many of the nurses were very nice.

One time close to Christmas, they did take us on a horse-driven sleigh ride. The other kids and I were having a good time on the sleigh when a nurse asked, "Okay, how many of you are ready to go home?" I was the only one who raised their hand. The nurse said to the other adults on the sleigh, "She thinks you mean to her own home. The other kids knew that we meant to the hospital."

Finally, the day came when the nurse said to me, "Your dad and mom are going to come and pick you up today." I was so excited I could hardly wait. I was able to walk that time, and I knew my parents would be so happy about it.

As the years passed, I was quite a sickly child. I had constant sore throats and swollen glands. At age twelve, my mother realized that I was limping more and more. The doctor determined that I needed to have a cord lengthening of my polio leg, which is my right leg. They performed the surgery at Children's Hospital in Buffalo. One night while in the hospital, I called the nurse because I had to go to the bathroom really bad to have a bowel movement. She brought me the bedpan. I tried for a long time but could not go. She came to get the bedpan and told me I was just looking for attention and to not bother her anymore. My problem was that my whole right side was affected when

I had polio, and even the muscles in my stomach did not function well. I had problems with constipation since I had polio. At that time, I made the decision that I was going to be a nurse and a good one and never hurt children.

Chapter 3

Going back to the time when I was seven and was really a skinny, unattractive child, I believed, I was chosen, from those in my first communion class, to recite the beautiful poem *Lovely Lady Dressed in Blue*. I recited this at the big Mother's Day breakfast. This boosted my self-image.

As I became an adult, I realized that these events when I was little and others in my youth would impact my whole life.

One day, when my younger brothers, who were four and five years younger than me, got into a lot of trouble, someone in the neighborhood took apart a greenhouse, which was made mostly of windows, and stacked them in piles. My brothers, with few friends, decided it would be fun to throw stones through and break all those windows. My father, who was very angry, said to them, "Okay, you're going to Father Baker's, and you're going to stay there." He had them pack their suitcases and get ready to leave.

My sister and I were sitting at the top of the stairs, sobbing, "Daddy, please don't take them. They will be good from now on."

My father loaded them into the car and drove for a while. He returned after a while with the boys and assured my sister and I that they had promised to be good from now on. My sister and I, years later, learned that my father and mother concocted this just to teach them a lesson.

Believe me when I say I was no angel growing up. Below are a few examples.

I had earned some money babysitting for neighbors, and I went and bought some candy. My little brother decided he wanted my candy, so he stole it from my hands and started to run. He ran in the back door and out the front door, with me chasing him. After about the second or third time, my brother put his arm through the glass in the front door. I won't go into the whole details, but it ended up him having sixteen stitches in the upper arm. As my mother knew it was an accident, she assured me that I was not in any real trouble. I remember feeling sorry that my brother had to have stitches in his arm.

My older brother Ronnie, who is about seventeen months older than me, and I are very close. We did everything together. He had a paper route, and I always helped him with it. When finishing the paper route, we would stop at the store and get a treat. Sometimes, he would treat me to a movie after I helped him with the route. This one time he said, "I want to be alone. I'm going to go to the movies by myself."

I said, "I want to go."

He started to run and climbed fences going through backyards, and I followed him every bit of the way. Finally, he gave up and said, "Oh come on, let's go to the movies."

When he was fifteen or sixteen, he was still letting me hang with his crowd, and they weren't always the best kids. They decided they wanted to build a raft or boat of some kind to put in the creek. To accomplish this, they were going to have to steal wood from a big barn that somebody had stored lumber in the upper part of it. He told me that I could not be with them and that I had to go home, and I said to him, "If you don't let me go, I'm going to tell Dad." They all agreed to let me be the lookout. I was happy as a clam. Just briefly, they accomplished building the boat. They put it into the creek where a dike was. They then rowed over to the other side where a big tree was. They hung a rope, to make a swing. Swinging from the tree, jumping into the water, and rowing the boat down the creek became our favorite activity that summer.

You would wonder why this behavior. We were all in Catholic school and knew right from wrong. Who knows? Side thought, my father was the first deputy sheriff in Genesee County and was now a city fireman.

Now on the nice side, my brother Ronnie was an altar boy for many years. I always accompanied him to church when it was his turn to serve. The priest who was always saying mass when Ron was serving one day gave me a little iron statue of the Sacred Heart, which I was very devoted to. He told me to say three Our Fathers and three Hail Marys every day for my vocation. He shared with me that when he was an altar boy, another priest, many years ago, gave him this little statue and asked for the same prayer situation that he was asking of me. I think he thought I was going to become a nun. I always treasured this statue and carried on this tradition into adulthood. Over the years, I observed my own family members and others whom I knew to see if there was anyone who looked like they might be interested in priesthood or other church vocations. No one seemed interested. A few years ago, my husband and I talked to the pastor of our own church and explained to him about the statue and that we felt that this statue should be passed on. Some of the altar boys at our church were older, and the question came up. "Have any of them shown interest in a vocation in the Church?" We told Father to use his best judgment and if he found someone to pass it on to, it was not necessary to let us know the name or any of the details if he wanted to keep it private. Unfortunately, shortly after this, he was assigned a different parish. We didn't ever learn whom the statue went to.

Please understand that we understood that we were not praying to the statue but to Jesus. Just like we have pictures of our family and when we look at the pictures, it helps us remember the person in the picture.

In ninth grade, I received an award. The DAR each year presented a student from the Batavia City School District with this award for excellence of social studies. My parents were really happy about this and proud of me. My teacher explained to me that it was my paragraph on the final exam that was the tiebreaker from the other students. This award was presented to me at the high school graduation that year. To this day, I can't remember what I wrote.

Chapter 4

Our engagement picture

HOW WE GROW

Our wedding picture

At age sixteen, like most girls of that age, I had become very interested in boys. My friends and I were over at the park watching a ball game between LeRoy boys and the Batavia boys. After the game of course, the girls were flirting a little bit with the guys from both teams. This one boy caught my eye, and I asked a friend who he was. He told me his name was Joe Condidorio. Months went by, and it was a couple of weeks before Christmas. A friend, who was a boy, asked me what I was asking Santa Claus for Christmas, and I replied, "I wouldn't mind having Joe Condidorio under my Christmas tree." I did not know at that time that Joe and he were friends. He told Joe what I had said. On New Year's Eve, there was a YMCA dance. Joe asked me to dance, and ever since, we have been together. We just celebrated sixty-nine years of marriage. Also when I was sixteen, I developed a swelling in my face along with a sore throat. My father took me to a throat specialist, who decided I should have my tonsils out. The doctor reported to my mother after the surgery that my tonsils had been buried and infected for many, many years and this was probably why I had sore throats for so many years as a young child. That year, I also had to have my appendix out.

In 1952, I graduated from high school and was accepted into Saint Mary's Hospital School Of Nursing in Rochester, New York. I started the program in September of 1952. Joe would come to see me about once a week with a car full of his friends. I would round up a few of the nursing students and the boys, and we would go out for supper. We had a great time. About six weeks into the program, I had an episode where I was completely paralyzed for only a few hours. After many tests and discussions, it was determined that I had hysterical paralysis, probably dating back to my childhood when I was away from home for so long. They informed my mother that they felt that I was not able to continue the program even though I was doing very well and excelling in the program. Of course, I was devastated.

I then decided to interview for a job at the Edith Hartwell Clinic in LeRoy, a facility for children with cerebral palsy. After the interview, the director told me I had a job if I wanted it. I was hired to be an aide in the education program. I loved the job, and I loved the children whom I was working with. The teacher was a wonderful young teacher, who helped me learn how to work with handicapped children and to help them do their best. Joe graduated a year after me and gave me a diamond ring on his graduation day. Joe had already secured a job at the LeRoy Machine Company. We went to talk to my father and mother about a wedding day and that we were thinking about April of the next year. My father asked us, "Why are you waiting so long?"

We looked at each other and asked each other, "Why are we waiting?" We decided to get married that year, which was 1953, and had a large Italian wedding. Mass was at 10:00 a.m. We had donuts for breakfast, and then we had a big dinner. It started with wedding soup and then pasta with meatballs and then chicken with potatoes and, of course, the salad. The custom in my husband's neighborhood at that time was that the women would get together and prepare the dinner and serve it. I should clarify that when you sent out an invitation for the wedding, people didn't all get invited to all parts of the wedding. Usually, family and close friends were invited to the full wedding, while others were invited to the church ceremony and then to the reception. The reception went from about 7:00 p.m. to 11:00 p.m. We had a great four-piece band, and people danced and had a lot of fun. We had homemade cookies, cookie cake, homemade pizza, and of course, all kinds of things to drink, wine, liquor, beer, and pop.

We left for the honeymoon, planned to go to New York, but the weather was bad, so we turned around. The weather was better going west, and so we went to Buffalo and spent the night in a motel, in their honeymoon suite. The next day, we went to New York. We had a wonderful time. I'm not going into details because it would take just too much time.

The next era of our life began, "the life of Joe and Florence Condidorio."

We decided to live with my mother-in-law in her apartment, as it had two bedrooms. She was alone, and it was good for all of us. Nine months and thirteen days later, we had our first baby, Gregory birth date September 10, 1954. We decided when we were in high school that when we had children, our first children would be named Gregory and then hopefully a girl named Darlene. We decided we didn't want to name our children after other people. A short time later, I became pregnant again, and we decided we needed a larger home. We purchased a home with my mother-in-law, and we turned it into a duplex, with my mother-in-law living upstairs and us downstairs. Fifteen months later, we had another baby, a girl, and named her Darlene birth date December 29, 1955. Joe began his endeavors of remodeling our downstairs apartment. It is important for all to understand that Joe did not know how to do any of the remodeling. His father died when he was two. His first endeavor was to build all new kitchen cabinets. He bought some books and proceeded to build the cabinets. They were beautiful.

Chapter 5

Jeffrey Joseph was born twenty-one months later on September 21, 1957. About a month after I had Jeffrey, I began bleeding severely with a high fever and was transported to the hospital in Batavia. The doctor performed a D&C as afterbirth had been left in. The next morning, the doctor informed me that if it weren't for penicillin, I would be dead. Fortunately, my mother-in-law and sister-in-law were there at the time I was having trouble and were able to take care of the four children who were left at home.

Over our early married years, Joe was so good in Math, I encouraged him to go to college. I offered to work before he started college to help with college tuition. I was hired by General Electric to work in the factory. I worked there for about nine or ten months before I got pregnant with Jeff. Joe started into college, a two-year business school at that time. He went to school all day for two years, even summer school, as that was built into the program. At 4:00 p.m. every day, for five days of the week, he reported to LeRoy Machine Shop and worked the 4:00 p.m. to 12:00 a.m. shift. As long as he made his quota of pieces for the day, he was allowed to spend the rest of the time doing his homework. Joe had been a smoker since he was fourteen. One day, after he completed his shift at the machine shop and they were going out for a hot dog, the discussion began with how much each of them smoke each day. Joe pulled out a pack of cigarettes that he had bought before he went to work that day. He discovered he had already smoked half the pack. He threw the pack of cigarettes on the table and said, "Here, anybody can have them. I quit." As an incentive, Joe started putting a quarter away in a dish, without my knowledge. One day, when I was looking in my china cabinet, I discovered this dish full of quarters, and it was overflowing. I thought we had hit it rich. I called to Joe and said, "Joe, I found this huge dish of quarters."

Joe responded, "I stopped smoking, and I put a quarter a day in this dish, which I would have spent on cigarettes."

I realized then that I had not been aware that Joe had stopped smoking. That made me realize that we had not been seeing much of each other because of all Joe's schooling and work.

Twenty-three months later, on August 10, 1957, we had another son. We were leaving the hospital when the nurse said to us, "You can't leave. You haven't named your baby."

Very quickly, Joe and I decided to name our new baby, Joseph James. The day Joe was supposed to take his final major exam was the day Joe was born. He waited till afternoon before he decided to come into this world. Of course, my husband remained with me for the full day. The next day, when Joe went to class, he asked the professor when he could take a makeup exam. The professor said that he would not have to take that exam as he already had a ninety-six percent average. Upon graduation, he was hired by

Eastman Kodak to work in the computer department. They were impressed that he was able to go to college, work full-time, and have a family.

Twenty-three months later, Patrick Joseph was born on December 20, 1960. At this time, I now had two children whom I was babysitting, my niece's son and a nephew's daughter. We had four boys sleeping in the big bedroom, and Darlene was still in the little bedroom. It was a good thing that Joe had turned the summer kitchen into our bedroom. We had a nice big yard outside that home, and we put in an above-ground pool, where our kids, the kids that I was taking care of, and some of the neighborhood kids would play in the water. We had a sandbox, with pails and shovels and trucks in it. Joe had plenty of room to throw around a ball around and teach them how to use a bat and all that kind of sports-related skills they would need as they grew older. Joe was still working at the racetrack in the evening, in Batavia, taking a quarter from each car that entered the parking lot. The track was operational for about four months out of the year. Joe started working there when Greg was a baby. This was another way to supplement our income. I had started, several years ago, to run what we called the toy parties. The toy company let me, as a demonstrator, buy toys at a cost. Then I would go out and demonstrate them at different homes, starting with our friend's homes. The person holding the toy party in their home would be able to buy the toys at a cost and also get a little commission when others who were at the party were buying toys at retail cost. It was a win-win situation. Many of us were able to give our children a really nice

Christmas with all the toys that we were getting at a cost. We also were making a little bit of cash on the side, because other people were buying toys at retail price and we would receive a commission on what they bought.

Chapter 6

Sixteen months later, Douglas Joseph was born on April 16, 1962. Now we had four boys sleeping in what was our old bedroom. We had moved into the new bedroom. Doug was put into the crib in Darlene's bedroom. Joe and I began to think about maybe we needed to look for something bigger in a home. Twenty months later, on December 17, Michael Joseph was born. Doug went into the big boys' room, and Mike went into the crib in Darlene's room. You can tell by now we were very good Catholics. We decided by now that we needed to build a house, and we started to design it. It would have six bedrooms, two-and-a-half baths, and much living space. On the top level, there would be four bedrooms, a large bath, a big kitchen and dining area, and a large living room. We decided that the only possible way to do this was to build an elevated ranch, utilizing both floors completely for living areas. Coming in from outside, in front of the house, walking into the garage up a few stairs, one would be in a mid-landing of the house. Also there would be the door coming in from the front of the house through the center of the house and into the mid-floor, choice being, up to the floor that was described above or down to the lower floor, which I will describe. Going down the central stairway to the right were two bedrooms, one-and-a-half baths, a large utility room that was also a second kitchen and laundry room, and a small furnace room. To the left from the stairs you would find a very large family room with a big marble fireplace; three huge glass doors leading out to the patio; a closet for coats, boots, and shelves; and a storage in the back, as well as a very large playroom, with a huge storage area. A friend of ours created the blueprints from our drawings. The bank approved us for a loan for what the builder was charging us and the cost of the land. We started building in the spring of 1965. Periodically, Joe and I and the kids would go to look at the house being built. One day, we went in, and there were no steps yet, but there was a ladder leading down from the top floor to the bottom floor. We were on the lower floor when we heard noise up above. Joe called up to see who was there. Two people from the neighborhood were up there. The one man asked, "Who is this house being built for?"

Joe answered, "For me."

He asked, "Where did you get the money?"

Joe answered, "At the bank. They have plenty of money."

No more was said by anyone.

On July 17, 1965, our second daughter, eighth child, was born, Beth Ann. I was asked during labor if I would mind if a group of students, from India, who were going to be nurses, could come in and observe the birth of my child. They selected me to ask since I had already given birth to seven babies. I agreed. At that point, I really didn't care if the whole world wanted to watch.

HOW WE GROW

Our first nine children

FLORENCE CONDIDORIO

Front of our new home

Back of our new home plus swimming pool

During these early years when we still lived on Church Street, we did have one accident. Our oldest son was pulling one of his younger brothers in a wagon, and it tipped over. We could tell the little one was injured, and we took him to the hospital. Sure enough, he had a broken arm. Of course, we all felt this was a big deal, not knowing what the future would bring. We decided to take a week's vacation that August, before moving into our new home in September. We rented a cottage over the border into Canada on Lake Erie. We always traveled with all our children, to any point at a time, laying down the second and third seats, covering the area with sleeping bags, and all the kids would sit Indian style. I would hold the baby in my arms. When we arrived at the cottage, I was appalled to learn that they had no hot running water. On the plus side, we were right on the beach, close to the water, so the kids could go out and play in the water and on the beach with us close by. Remember I had a newborn baby and I felt the kids needed baths once in a while. We heated many pans of water for baths and for formula. The kids and Joe had a wonderful time. I was completely exhausted and glad to return home. We moved into our new home at 38 East Ave. at the end of August 1965. Many of our friends and relatives helped us move the large pieces of furniture. The older kids had the responsibility of moving all their own personal things into their new rooms. Of course, there was much excitement for the kids. They had seen the rooms empty while they were being built. To actually move into their room with only two beds was unbelievable to them. The boys had been sleeping in a room with six twin beds. We all slept in our new home that night.

When we designed this new home, we also included these special features. The home was so large that we decided to have them build a built-in vacuum cleaner system. Also I knew that I would need something built in to help me communicate with the kids, as the house was so large, upstairs and downstairs, in the garage, and at the patio. We had them install an intercom system so we could communicate with the kids in any of the rooms, even outside. This also allowed me to listen in to what was going on in other parts of the house. My mother and father painted the whole house inside and out, except for staining the woodwork.

My father, uncle, and brother-in-law decided to take on the responsibility of putting in a double-wide concrete driveway. The garage was a two-car garage with extra depth, attached to the house. There was a back door of the garage that led out to a stairway going down to the patio. The length of the patio was about seventy feet, and the width was about eight feet. At each end of the patio was a retaining wall about three feet high that you could actually sit on. Another brother-in-law offered to make lined drapes for each of the room's windows, including draw drapes for the three large door windows in the family room.

It took us about a month to get fully moved in. The other children whom I was caring for came shortly after we moved into our new home. Our children, along with the other children, really enjoyed having all the space for the toys, playing together, running up and down the stairs, riding bikes on the patio, and playing in the large sandbox that Joe had built for them.

HOW WE GROW

Family room

Sand box

I applied for my certification for the Condidorio Day Care Center. After all the red tape, I was granted the certification. I could no longer take children under 2; as a requirement, one full-time person was needed for each two children under 2. At this time, I had four children just under 2, but they made an exception because these little boys were so close to 2. Our ninth child, John Joseph, was born October 27, 1967.

Joe began working again at the Batavia Downs Racetrack, sometime after we moved into the new home. Since he now had a degree in accounting, he was placed in the calculating room. The job at the racetrack was seasonal. This was in addition to his full-time job at Kodak. I also continued my toy parties around Christmastime. Eventually, I also began having clothing parties. They were called Beeline parties as the clothing were from the Beeline Clothing Co.

The extra money earned helped us with our needs for our large family.

In 1967, we decided that instead of trying to take a vacation, we would invest in a large swimming pool. A friend of Joe's, whose father sold and installed pools, was contacted by Joe. He agreed to do the digging and installation of the pool, except for the liner. Joe would have to provide adult men to help put in the liner under his supervision. A white cap was around the edge of the pool, and then there was five or six twelve-inch blocks of concrete all the way around the pool. Around the outside of the blocks was installed a chain-link fence, which had a gate on the side of the house. This gate was always locked with a padlock, unless the pool had supervision. When the day care center was in operation, I was mandated by the State to have a certified lifeguard / swim instructor available to act as a lifeguard.

Over these years, many happenings in our life occurred. In 1964, Joe was voted in for a two-year term as a councilman on the LeRoy Village Board. At one point in time, the board members and the councilmen attended the Conference of Mayors in New York City. Joe tells the story, when flying on the plane, the plane encountered some bad weather and they had to fly around New York City before landing. Joe's vertigo kicked in, and he was pretty sick on the plane. When they finally landed, he went right to bed, cutting his evening short. The next day, they attended many meetings with people from all over New York State. They also had some time to do sightseeing. One day, during a snowstorm, Joe was riding on the snow plow, to help with the visibility, when they received a call: East Avenue needed to be cleared as there was an injured child. When the report came over that it was 38 East Avenue, Joe realized it had to be one of his own children. The child had fallen and hit his head on the fireplace and needed stitches. The child was transported back home after getting his stitches, and all was okay.

During another snow storm, the Thruway was closed, and a young couple was stranded. Joe asked them if they would like to come and spend the night at our house. They drove over with Joe and got settled in. Joe returned to the Village Hall. Shortly after, a couple with three little kids came into the Village Hall, as they had no place to go.

The father was in the service, and the family was coming from Guam. His father, who was dying, lived in Ithaca. Joe called and asked if I thought we could handle them. Of course, I said yes. They soon showed up at the house with Joe. That night, the kids all slept on sleeping bags in the playroom, and the adults had the bedrooms. The kids, the three little towheads, and our dark-haired kids, at bedtime, all knelt down in the playroom and said their prayers together. Food was not a problem, as we always had lots of cereals, eggs, and food in the freezer. I can't even tell you what we ate, but I knew everybody was full and nobody was complaining. Our little guests had never seen snow. The next morning, we bundled the little guests up in snowsuits, and our older children took them out to play in the snow. It was a great experience for all our families. That afternoon, the Thruway opened up, and all our guests were on their way. A short time later, we heard from both families. The couple, newly married, sent a little gift and said they couldn't wait to have children of their own after their experience with all our kids and our little guests. The other couple explained to us that they had been Catholic and had fallen away from the church. After seeing the children praying together, they decided it was important for them to return to the church and raise their children as Catholics.

Many of our children attended Holy Family School. Every year, each class had an end-of-the-year picnic. We hosted each of our children's classes for their picnics. The children would come with their bathing suits and with teacher or nun supervision. Joe cooked dozens and dozens of hot dogs. We can't remember what the other food was or how it got there. This occurred every year that the children were at Holy Family School.

Our boys also played Little League Baseball. After all the playoff games, we hosted pool parties for all of our son's teams who were playing baseball. Joe again cooked many, many hot dogs, while the kids swam in the pool before they ate.

The helpers whom I had, especially at pre-lunchtime and into nap time, were instructed when they lay the little ones down for their nap to always stay with them for a few minutes and give them a hug and a kiss so they feel comfortable. I was allowed to use the six twin beds, two to a room, for naps instead of cots. I did have to provide an individual sheet for each bed before the child lay on it. One of the helpers was taking college courses and was relaying this protocol to her instructor. The instructor told the class that it was rare to see this kind of caring for children in a day care. The next day, my helper told me about the incident. Of course, I was pleased at this.

Two inspectors would appear at any time, without notice, to do an evaluation of the day care program. This one time, I was seated in the family room with them discussing the program, and one of my little guys, about three or four years old, came walking down the front stairs. He asked, "Aunt Florence, can I come and sit on your lap?"

"Sure, Tommy, come over here," I replied.

The inspectors were surprised. The inspector said the kids seem so comfortable here. Surprising to me, I never received a report from the State about my day care program.

At one point in time, Joe discussed with me that he would like to have a full-size pool table in the family room.

We realized that it would be one more activity that the older kids could have and a new life skill that they could learn. Joe ordered the table and set it up, and on one wall behind the table, he put up the accessories. We also had a foosball table, which one of my children had asked for, for Christmas. All the kids loved to play that also.

By 1968, I was caring for about six or seven little ones during the school year. During the summer, my enrollment of kids could be ten or twelve plus my own. My number of helpers was determined by the number of children I had enrolled.

After the first year of moving into our new home and having children that I was taking care of besides my own, I knew I had to have someone help clean the house, so I hired a cleaner. She came one day a week.

After having the day care in our home for about three or four years, we decided we needed to do something about the milk situation. It was hard to pour that many milk glasses, especially in the summertime. We spoke to a milkman, and he suggested we get a tabletop refrigerator. He would deliver large containers of milk and put them in the refrigerator on the table in our utility room on the lower floor. By raising the handle, milk would come out of the spout and into the glass. Plastic glasses where right next to the machine. To the kids, this was now the milk machine. The kids loved it. Amazingly, today, the children, who are now adults, still come back and talk about the milk machine.

Joe and I felt so blessed to have such a wonderful home, children, family, and income. Every Sunday, Joe and I would dress the kids up and pile them into the car, and we would be off to the 9:30 a.m. mass. One day, we all piled into the car to go to mass, and I said, "Oh, wait a minute. We forgot the baby." I always got the baby ready first and put him in his crib. Of course we went back in and got the baby and brought him out. As our family grew, we took up more than one whole pew. Night prayers were said as a family group when the kids were young. I taught social Christianity over the years to both elementary-age kids and high school kids. Bath time was a production for Joe and I. We had three or four little ones in the tub at one time. I washed them, and Joe dried them. It was always a fun time. The older children of course took their own showers or baths.

As our kids were in the Catholic school, we felt obligated to help with fundraising. We became the chairpersons for decorating for the Cherry Blossom Ball. We became a little crazy. We decided to take chicken wire and hang it from the ceiling. Before it was hung, we wove in sprigs we had cut from the trees, which were covered by rose buds made from pink crepe paper. We also fashioned a bridge, which couples would have to cross to come into the dancing area. The hall looked beautiful, and we were able to use the same decorations for many years. It certainly was a lot of work.

When all the kids were young, we always had Sunday as a family day and always spaghetti or shell macaroni for lunch, our main meal. As the kids got older and some were married and had children, we continued this tradition with our grandchildren. Our young children and grandchildren continued running up one staircase and down the other as the adults continued to sit at the table and discuss their current lives. By accident, we learned that the older children were passing the young grandchildren from the laundry chute upstairs in the bathroom to the laundry chute down in the utility room. Our older children sitting at the table, as young adults, confessed that they also used to do this with your younger siblings. Thank goodness the chutes had large holes. I think we put an end to that little fun activity, but I would not swear to it.

Most of our children also took ballet lessons. LeRoy was blessed to have a prima ballerina from Europe who was our dance instructor. We learned that professional football players were now taking ballet lessons to increase their skills needed to be top-notch football players. That was our incentive to have our boys take ballet. Our oldest daughter of course was taking ballet as she was our little girl and we loved seeing her doing her dances. Every year, our dance teacher put on a marvelous performance of *The Nutcracker.* One of our sons always played the little boy in the performance. Our daughter always danced several dances. Over the years, the dance instructor decided to have adults learn to dance ballroom dances, jitterbugs, rhombus, etc. Joe and I, along with some of our friends, were delighted over the new dances that we would learn. Ballroom dancing was always one of our favorite activities, and sometimes, we would be out dancing one night a week. Occasionally, we would put music on, and we would be dancing in our living room. One time, a neighbor across the street kidded us about watching us dance from his porch. Periodically, we continued to play canasta with our card group.

Other memories were not so much fun. One of our sons who had stitches in his chin caused by a flip he was doing on the diving board had just healed. The kids were out playing baseball, and he got hit by the bat. His face was starting to swell, so I called the doctor and explained the situation. I told him that one of the other boys also had a problem and his knee was swelling, also that one of the boys who, a couple of weeks ago hurt his arm and had X-rays but it was determined it was not broken, was now still having pain. He said he would call the X-ray department at the hospital and let them know that I was bringing all three boys in for X-rays. It turned out, the boy with the injured arm did have a broken arm. The other two did not have any breaks, but they needed to be iced frequently.

Of course over the years, our children and the day care children came down with the same childhood diseases, measles, mumps, chickenpox, strep throats, colds, etc. Sometimes, I wished I had stock in calamine lotion. As the kids were healing from chickenpox, I felt like I was spending a lot of time plastering calamine lotion all over their bodies.

Thank goodness the day care children had very few accidents over the course of many years. One little boy who had braces on his legs to keep his legs apart could not go into the pool. He was sitting on the retaining wall, watching the kids swim, with me standing right next to him. He slid off the wall, and I just couldn't catch him. He landed on the concrete patio. He needed to have a few stitches on his face. I called his mom, who came right over and took him to the doctors. We all agreed it was no big deal.

One summer, LeRoy decided to build a swimming pool to enhance its summer program. They were having a fundraiser to raise money for the new pool. Our swimming instructor had the idea that we could be part of that. We decided to have a penny carnival to raise money for the pool. We made stuffed animals with the kids helping us. She cut and sewed the pieces together, and kids stuffed and sewed the little hole that they needed to fill it with. These were used as prizes. I can't recall all the little games we designed, but one of them was throwing the bean bags into a hole to win prizes. On the penny carnival day, many kids showed up with their money to play the games. We raised over $100 and donated it to the pool fund.

Another time, Joe had a great idea. "Let's get the kids a dirt bike." We had the perfect place to have it. We built our home at the end of a paved street, East Ave. Where our street ended, a dirt street continued on, and it was quite long and curved, taking you over to the next street. Kids called it the bumpy road. At one point of the bumpy road, there was a horse path, which took you past a little creek. Occasionally, we would take the kids for a walk down by the creek. The bumpy road was a perfect place for the kids to ride a dirt bike. Joe purchased the bike and taught the older kids and the older day care kids to ride it. Needless to say, it was a favorite activity, and the kids did learn to take turns on it. Only one time did an accident happen on it. One of our boys was playing Evel Knievel and went face first over the front of the bike. He broke several teeth when they went through his lip. His cousin from Cleveland who was visiting us happened to be at the end of the bumpy road and carried him home. He was taken to the doctors for stitches and later to the dentist, who set a plan for taking care of the teeth.

Christmas was always very special. On Christmas Eve, we would always go to my parents' house with our family. Also present would be all my siblings and their children. We would be there for supper about 5:00 p.m. and open presents for the children from the grandparents, and then my mother would go to the piano, and everybody would be standing around, singing all the Christmas carols. About 8:00 p.m., we would leave to go back to LeRoy. Joe's sisters, their families, and his mother would be waiting for us at our home. In the early years, we would not eat until after midnight mass. There were mountains of presents from each other to be opened. Some of the young adults would be sitting on the stairs joking around. The kids were only interested in opening presents. After midnight mass, all the adults would be eating. The little ones were fed earlier and then laid down to sleep. Festivities ended about three in the morning, and then everyone would return to their own homes.

Our night was very short as Santa still had to bring all of our children's gifts under the tree. Our children were early risers on Christmas, and we expected them to be up about 7:00 a.m. They all knew they had to come and get Mom and Dad up before they could get to the tree to see their presents. The first ones went to wake up their siblings.

During Christmas Day, Joe's family would return to our home about 1:00 p.m. We would make homemade raviolis before Christmas and freeze them. Also we would make homemade spaghetti sauce, with meatballs and other meats, a couple of days before. Joe's family would bring the other goodies that we had for dinner plus deserts. One summer day, Joe came home from being out and said to me, "I think there are more kids here than usual." He went out to count the kids and came back and said, "You know there are thirty-seven kids here today." We realized that outside there were our ten kids—the daycare kids, our kid's friends, and also the neighborhood kids. Some were in the pool, some were out playing baseball, and some were in the sandbox. Of course, we did have our lifeguard, myself, and another aide who were here observing and watching all of what was going on.

As the older kids became teenagers, they let us know they were tired of coming home from school every day to a household of little kids. As we thought about this, I said to Joe, "I would like to go to college." I explained that I would either get a degree in nursing or in education. As usual, Joe was very supportive of this idea. He suggested that I take one course at GCC just to see if I thought I could do it. As I was always good in math, he suggested I take a math course. I decided to take a modern math course, as that was what was being taught in school. I could always use this course to help my children with the modern math they were being taught. I received an A in the course, and we decided I would start attending college. We decided on an education degree instead of a nursing degree, as we wanted me to be home during the summers and holidays with the kids. I was entitled to free tuition and cost of books due to my problem with effects of polio.

Now we have 10

I was accepted into the Geneseo education program for K through 6. I continued a small day care center for the first two years of my education. If I had day classes, I would hire someone to come in during those periods of time. Most of the time, I would enroll in early morning and some night classes. I would go to bed at the same time as my children and get up about three in the morning to work on my homework. Needless to say, none of this could have occurred without my husband picking up so much slack and also the older kids helping out more. All the kids were used to helping out at home. From the time they were little, they had to make their own beds and help clean the kitchen before they went to school in the morning. One time, one of our children, attending kindergarten, told his nun that he would have to clean the whole house and the kitchen before he came to school. Laughing, one day, she relayed this to me and said, "I won't believe everything he tells me if you don't believe everything he tells you about me."

Another time, it was relayed to me that my oldest son was invited over to a friend's house. The father, a widower, said to my son, "I want you to tell my kids what you have to do before you leave the house to go to school." Apparently he was having trouble getting his kids to help out at home.

After a little over a year in college, I found out I was pregnant again, for our tenth child. Just after completing my second year of college in the middle of May, Thomas Joseph was born on June 7, 1971. It was tough that last semester, walking those Hills in Geneseo as big as a house. As we hadn't had a baby in the house for about five years, he became everybody's baby. When I resumed my education in the fall, my oldest daughter was also in college. If she or I both had classes at the same time, one of us would take him to day care. Joe and the kids were still all pitching in to help. All through this time, we continued to have a cleaning woman come in, which was a big help.

In my education classes, professors always stressed the fact that children should have as many experiences as possible. I saw an advertisement that they were looking for little girls in the Genesee region to participate in a beauty pageant. One would be chosen after an interview process to be entered into the State pageant. Our younger daughter at the time was six, and I decided to let her interview for this program. Several weeks later, I was called and told that our little girl had been selected to represent this area. A local children's store donated a party dress and a sports outfit for her to model. The week-long pageant took place at a western New York college. When we arrived, we were assigned a room in one of the dormitories. We found out there were four levels of competition. Our daughter's category was called Miss La Petite and did not require a talent. The other categories were broken down by age and required a talent. The week was spent with our daughter having many interviews, lessons in modeling, and practices walking down the runway. We learned that she was competing against children who were professional models from as far away as New York City. On the final day of the competition, many of our relatives showed up to see the pageant. When the winners were announced, they announced the Miss La Petite first, and our daughter won the title. The host and hostess put a red cape on our daughter's shoulders, a crown on her head, and a dozen roses in her arms. She then proceeded to walk down the runway, get to the end, do her pivot, and walk back. It was amazing to see this small six-year-old with so much confidence. She won her and I a trip to New Orleans to participate in the national pageant. Our daughters, Joe, and I flew to New Orleans when it was time. She did not place in the national pageant, but we all had a wonderful time, as we experienced much of New Orleans during that week. The next year, she returned to the State pageant and had to crown the new Miss La Petite.

These are little memories from my days in college. I was taking a behavior management course, and the program was very much against any type of physical contact for discipline. From my experience with all the children I came in contact, a little crack on the behind once in a while was acceptable. I brought this thought to the professor's attention. He asked, "Do you have children?"

I replied, "Yes, I do. I have ten children."

He looked at me amusingly and replied, "I guess I have to defer to you."

The class started to laugh. In reality, when we were raising children, we did believe in spanking, but never in anger. We even did use a belt on a behind once in a while.

I received my first D ever in a Political Science course. I was devastated, almost crying in the class, when I received my paper back. My take of the government at that time was we had a great government, and I wrote about all the good things that the government did. One of the students sitting near me realized what a problem I was having. Trying to console me, he said, "The professor's a jerk." Years later, I began to realize that what the professor was trying to do was to get us to think about what was wrong with the government and how we could make the government better.

I graduated in 1973. The older children, my husband, and I loaded into the car with me in my graduation gown. I was so proud to have them see me walk across the stage and get my diploma.

As was always the case, my parents and Joe's mother, all through the years, were always there to help us along the way with babysitting or anything else we needed.

It was now time to look for a job. I put my application in many local schools and had several interviews. I was interviewed at the Batavia City School. The principal who interviewed me had several of his own children attending the New York State School for the Blind (NYSSB) in Batavia. They were born with a congenital disease that lead to blindness. Shortly after that, I received a call from the principal at the New York State School for the Blind. He informed me that he had gotten my application from the principal at the Batavia City School. They were looking to fill a position called Dean of Students. Requirements were a bachelor's degree in education and experience supervising people. Since I had people working for me in my day care center, that was the experience I needed. Shortly after, I was notified that I had the job if I wanted it.

The position was a department head position, supervising all aspects of the residential program, staff, transportation, and supervision of all the children and their welfare.

Early September, I attended the first orientation meeting with all the staff of the school. There was a new department head of education and a new psychologist. We were introduced to the rest of the staff. That day, I had a meeting with the former residential department head, who filled me in on many aspects of the staff, the students, and the program itself. The next day, I spent time with the residential staff, learning a little bit about the program before the children started arriving. My staff seemed nice and willing to work for the best interest of the kids. I was excited to meet the students.

At this time, there were over a hundred students at the school. They were considered normal blind kids. Most of them did not have any other major disability. In the months following the start of my employment, some of the things that were going on in the residential program caused me to be concerned. There were very few toys available for the kids to play with. The children were away from their families for six weeks at a time. My experience as a child away from home made me very sensitive to what the children might be experiencing being away from homes for such long periods of time. Punishment could include spankings with a belt, or if a child mislaid a sock or other clothing, they would be told to hold the piece of clothing in their hand and stand by their bed for ten minutes. I felt the schedules of the staff, if altered, could be much more productive. The first issue I tackled was the punishment situation. The new psychologist and I sat down and decided how we wanted this to be changed. There would be no more spankings or the socks or other clothing items protocol. We were promoting positive reinforcement. I also noticed that the education program staff would be teaching daily living skills totally different from the residential staff. This was not in the best interest of the students. Teachers in the education program would instruct their aides that consistency in teaching each student was important. Residential houseparents, as was their title, did not have people to help them. It became obvious that the residential staff would benefit from a training program. I met with the superintendent of the school to discuss my observations. Starting with what I felt was the easiest, I requested a budget for the residential program so we could start buying some toys that would enhance the children's lives. Play is children's work. I then explained that the consistency between the education program and the residential program was really necessary. I requested money to be able to purchase a curriculum for the residential staff that I could teach. He asked me to present a budget for these items to him. He was happy I was getting that involved that early in my position. When I discussed with him the problem of children being away from their homes for six weeks and changing the schedule of the houseparents, he informed me that Albany had set these in place and that he didn't think they could be changed. I was happy that at least a couple of these things could be changed immediately. The other items I would continue working on. I submitted the budget that he had asked for, and he found the money for these items. Soon the children had new toys to play with in the dormitories. As the school year was almost over, the curriculum wasn't purchased until the following year.

The new education coordinator and I became good friends over the first year, discussing the programs and our goals for the future. Neither of us worked summer school, so we had plenty of time to sit by my pool with our children and discuss some of the issues. We decided to have the education aids and the houseparents switch positions for an hour or two periodically. This would make them more aware of how the students were being taught in the school, what was happening in the dorm, common problems that all encountered, and the understanding of the positions in each program. This was implemented the following year, and most staff were receptive to it. We were happy to see how the two staff complemented each other and communicated with each other with regard to the children. We were also able to implement the houseparent curriculum. This was taught before the kids came to the dorms from school.

Several years after I started my position, the superintendent left. The acting superintendent, who had been in a different position, was open to my suggestion about getting kids home every weekend. Fortunately, I had been working on my plans on how to accomplish this. Since I was also the transportation coordinator, I had become very familiar with how this all worked. I knew the transporters well. I realized that the children from the Albany area and north of Albany would need a different type of transportation. The length, back and forth, every weekend, would be too much for the children. I had contacted some small airline companies and asked if they would be interested in transporting blind children from Batavia to their area and back on the weekend. They said they would be. All details still were not in place. We needed to show the State that they would be saving money by not having students here on the weekend. The school districts were responsible for the cost of students traveling back and forth to school for their education. The State would save money by not having to feed the kids on the weekends. Also no residential staff would be needed on the weekends. The acting superintendent presented this to Albany, and they agreed. Next, I worked with the current transporters of the students, set up routes with the small airlines, and dealt with school districts, parents, and staff before this all happened. There were several issues about this, but in the end, it did occur. Some of my own residential staff were upset because they were going to lose some overtime pay that they were getting working weekends.

I assured them that over time, they would be able to make this up by the training they were getting. We would then ask the State for an upgrade in their pay. Several years after I was hired, all children were going home every weekend to be with their families. To this day, the children still go home every weekend.

At this time, I had also revamped the whole schedule for all the houseparents. More staff was placed where they were most needed, fewer staff when children were in bed, and staff time for more training was accomplished. After several years of training, the staff were given an upgrade, from a grade 7 to a grade 9. Their titles were changed from houseparents to child care aide 1. This meant more money in their checks every week.

I also requested from the administration that they allow two of the child care aide 1 to move to a supervisory position, child care aide 2. This would give me the opportunity to get more information about the direct care of the students, as I did not have the time to be in the dorms all the time.

Chapter 7

Over the first half of the twenty years that I worked at the School for the Blind, we had many experiences both at NYSSB and continued to have them at home.

Joe got a call from a high school classmate of his. He was taking his Boy Scout troop to the New England area. He had been to our home before, and he knew that we had a large patio. He asked if he could stop with the Boy Scouts overnight and they could all sleep on the patio. Joe said to him that it was fine but to let him know when they were coming. Several weeks later, Joe got a call from his friend and set a date for them to arrive. When they arrived, they expected to sleep on the patio, but Joe had other plans. Joe insisted that they bring their sleeping bags in and sleep on the family room floor. The next morning, we had some breakfast, and they were on their way.

About four years after I started at NYSSB, I became pregnant again. No one was told except my husband, as our oldest son was going to get married soon. We did not want to take away from the excitement of the upcoming wedding. When I was about three months along, I had a miscarriage and was taken to the hospital. My son, who was getting married, had been to see me that morning, and I was fine. He called that afternoon; the phone was answered by one of my other sons. He asked to speak to me. The younger brother said that I wasn't home, I was in the hospital, and I had had a miscarriage. The older brother said to him, "Stupid, you can't have a miscarriage unless you're pregnant."

The younger brother said, "She was."

This was relayed to me by the older brother when he came to see me. The whole situation was then explained to the older brother.

At times we would pack the NYSSB students into the school bus and bring them to our home to swim for a little while in the afternoon. The residential staff would accompany and supervise them. Some of our own children and their friends or neighbors kids would act as buddies for the blind kids in the pool. It was a great experience for all involved.

I remember the first year I was there and the new staff were meeting with some of the students and the students were playing games on us. They put a blindfold on me and told me I had to find my office, which was up one floor. We were in the basement. My sense of direction has always been terrible. I ended up in a telephone booth around the corner from my office. They came to find me and led me back downstairs. Of course, the students were all laughing.

I received a call from a mother of one of our students one Friday, going home day. She informed me that she did not want her daughter anymore and if I sent her home on the bus, she would not be there to receive her. I had no choice but to make arrangements for her daughter to stay on that weekend. Normally, I would take the child to my home, but we had plans for the weekend. I contacted a friend of mine who had a foster child at the school and asked if it would be possible for her to take this beautiful five-year-old high-functioning, very personable, blind girl for the weekend.

She agreed to do this. Both the little girl and the lady and her family, who took care of her, had a wonderful time. The following week, I worked with the Social Services in our county and the child's county and the child's mother. Her mother was determined that she still did not want this child. Social Services in both counties finally resolved the issue, and the child was placed up for adoption. The adoptive parents turned out to be the family she spent the weekend with.

As time went on, I was in constant communication with the adoptive parents. Both the family and the little girl were very happy. Just recently, about forty years after this all occurred, my husband met a member of the adoptive family and inquired about the little girl. He was told that the stepmother had passed away several years ago and the little girl was now living with her stepsister and her family. All were very happy. By that time I had several new names, the students called me Mrs. C, as they had trouble with Condidorio, and the staff called me Flo.

The residential staff that I supervised were extraordinary. They went far and beyond what was expected of them. These are some of the examples:

Each year in June, they had a prom dance for the kids with a band. Some of these staff members went out and solicited from the community beautiful gowns for all the girls to wear. They went to the local tuxedo store who provided tuxedos for all of the boys. The night of the prom when many of the parents were there, some were in tears when they saw their beautiful blind children in gowns and tuxedos, dancing.

When they identified a need for one of the kids, the staff found a way to provide for that child to have whatever they needed.

They were creative in providing new and different activities for the students in the afternoon and evenings.

These staff were willing to help in anything that was needed for the students even if it meant doing things out of their job description.

One day, I was walking from the top floor to the first floor in the administration building. Older students were walking up the stairs. One of the teenage boys bumped into me. He commented, "You're no Dolly Parton," and continued walking up the stairs. I was totally shocked but laughing to myself. I learned from other staff and students that this was something the teenage boys often did, bumping on purpose into the girls and female staff members. I guess that was one way of seeing what the bodies of students and staff looked like.

In our home, things were pretty busy. On weekends during football season, we would usually go to one or two football games for the kids. We were now up to five or six. There were three levels of little teams, plus modified, JV and varsity. Some years, we had boys on all the teams. After many years, one of our boys even played college football. Besides that, our children always participated in Little

League Baseball. Our oldest daughter was taking ballet one or two times a week. Our younger daughter was big in gymnastics, sometimes practicing for three or four days a week in Niagara Falls. On weekends, we would go to gymnastics competitions anywhere in the State.

As time went on, I realized that there was another area that the older students at NYSSB were having trouble with. They were blind, and they couldn't see how each other was developing physically. I learned that there was not a program at NYSSB to teach them human development and sexuality. I sent for a curriculum on human development, set up separate classes for the older boys and girls, and began teaching them, using the curriculum. I borrowed a mannequin from a local store so they could at least feel the development of what girls go through. Unfortunately, I couldn't find a male mannequin with male genitalia. In class one day, one of the fifteen-year-old girls said to me, "Mrs. C., you know what, I really want to know what guys' balls feel like." I was shocked, to say the least. I told her that I would try to get something that would give her an idea of what these boys balls felt like. I relayed this story, when I got home, to my husband and my older kids. Of course, they laughed. Then I started my creative thoughts, *how do I create a penis and balls to at least resemble the real thing?* I ended up taking two nuts, encasing them in some cotton balls and covering them with some Saran wrap. Then I made the penis with some material. I made a pouch and suspended the penis and balls from that, using a narrow ribbon. This silly thing did somewhat satisfy the girls' curiosity. I explained to the girls that it wasn't exact but it was kind of what they felt like. The staff at the school got wind of this and were shown my model, and they laughingly called it Flo's Christmas ornament. As a joke, someone hung it on the Christmas tree.

Our oldest daughter, in her senior year, was selected to represent her school in the Junior Miss contest. She received the congeniality award as she was so helpful to all the other contestants. As her talent, she performed a beautiful ballet dance. She continues to maintain this helpful demeanor throughout her life with family members and friends.

Joe coached the senior division youth football team for several years. I served on the executive Board of Independent Living for many years.

As our grandchildren turned six or seven, I decided that I should take them shopping for their birthday presents and Christmas presents—no parents allowed. We usually headed out on the Thruway to Market Place Mall. They could put things in a cart, and then at the end of our trip, they would have to decide what they really wanted out of that cart. They were given a dollar amount, and I helped them with the math.

When we were shopping for Christmas presents, they were told that they had to look surprised when they opened their gift on Christmas. The first trip started out with two girl cousins. As the years passed, the numbers of grandchildren continued to grow and grow and grow. I would take them three or four at a time shopping. Later on, I used an electric cart, as I couldn't walk the malls. The car had a motorized lift in the trunk to accommodate the cart. The older kids easily learned how to help get it in and out of the car. They always decided where we were going to have lunch. One time, when the first cousins I took shopping became teenagers and we were Christmas shopping, they said, "Grandma, we need to go look for something. We'll be right back." I sat on my scooter and waited for a short time, and soon they returned. We had finished shopping, and now were returning to the car. Before I started the car, they said to me, "Grandma, we bought you a present." They handed me a bag containing a bright pink thong. I looked at them and started laughing and said thanks. On Christmas Eve, when we got together to celebrate Christmas, I appeared with my party clothes on and took them away from the group. I pulled my slacks down a little bit so they could see that I was wearing the pink thong, over my panties, of course. We were all laughing hysterically, and some of the group asked what was so funny. We did share the story with some of them, who also thought it was very funny.

One time when I had four of the young teenage boys shopping, I looked in the store window, and guess what I saw: they were standing, posed like mannequins. They did come down finally and continued shopping. Another time when I took these boys shopping, I took the wrong turn off the Thruway. I said to the boys, "Well, I guess we're going to shop in Buffalo." We all laughed at that. I wasn't sure where the mall was, but I was sure we could find it. We did after a few tries. As the kids will tell you, this wouldn't be the first time that we got lost. On the shopping trips, each grandchild had to have a little turn riding on my scooter before we loaded it into the car.

One day, the superintendent and principal took me out to lunch. After lunch, they asked if I would consider being the department head for education instead of the department head for the residential program. After discussing the pros and cons with them, I decided to make the change. The current department head of education was causing many problems for the teachers and program. She treated all her staff very poorly, belittling them, interfering with their teaching methods, and lowering their ability to supervise their school aides. As the new education department head, I knew that if the teachers were given back the freedom to use the skills that they learned when they were receiving their degree in education, the program could quickly be returned to the excellent program it had been. The teaching staff not only had their degrees in education, but many of them had degrees in special education. Over a two-year period, I observed the classrooms and the operations of it many times, did the evaluation of the teachers each year, and encouraged their creativity. After teachers received permission to run their classrooms and supervise their aides and their self-esteem was returned, the program returned to the excellent program it had been. At this point, I requested that I be returned to the residential department head position. This request was granted, and a new department head for education was hired.

I was anxious to get back to the residential program. I had observed over the two years that I did not supervise it that this program had deteriorated. The staff morale was way down, the creativity and interest in the students' welfare was not what it was, the energy level was down, self-esteem was down, etc. The staff was as glad to see me back as I was to see them. It didn't take very long to get it back to where it had been, as the staff was happy to see the program blossom again.

Chapter 8

About ten years after my employment at NYSSB began, blind children and children with other handicapping conditions were being mainstreamed into the public school. Blind multi-handicapped children who were originally being taught at home or did not have a program were now eligible to come to New York State School for the Blind (NYSSB). These new programs started slowly. Some of our students were now going to the public school, and we were beginning to take in the students with multiple handicaps. The new criterion for us was that the student had to be legally blind and have one other handicapping condition. After several years, some of the teachers began leaving because they didn't feel equipped to teach the blind children with other handicapping conditions. Some of our new children were deaf-blind, orthopedically impaired and blind, mentally impaired and blind, etc. As there was no time to really train the staff, both educational and residential, programs were then set up to accommodate the training. Some of the training consisted of learning sign language, how to lift students without hurting yourself or them, behavior management, etc. All the staff, including administration, education, residential, and dining room, had training to some degree. It soon became known to all that the residential facilities were not adequate. Some of the students on the second floor were orthopedically impaired, and it was very difficult for them to come down to the first floor. The fire department came in and showed the staff how they could move the kids from the second floor to the first floor by placing them on a blanket and moving them down the stairs. An outside small elevator was installed, moving between the ground and the second floor. It could hold a student and staff with the student's equipment. Another problem was the students had to leave the dormitory and go outside to get to their classroom or the dining room. As we received more of the orthopedically impaired students at the school, all involved realized that we needed a new building, which was handicapped accessible. The State started building the new dormitory soon after this. This was connected to the administration building by a tunnel. When it was completed, many of the students moved into that new building. One of the dormitories remained open for older students who were not orthopedically impaired. Only one of the older buildings was kept open. It was Park Lewis Hall. It was a challenge, but soon, all students were moved to their appropriate dormitories.

Sometime after this, the State decided they wanted us to consider an eight-bed intermediate care program. The superintendent asked if I would help out in starting this program and then consider running it. We would be able to hire a recreational therapist to be used in our program and the intermediate care program, an additional psychologist, a secretary, and new residential staff. I told him I would help with the starting of the program but really wasn't interested in running it. The state had assigned a consultant for these new programs, called ICFs, across the State. I began meeting with her on a regular basis. She was very knowledgeable and helpful. I interviewed people for the recreational therapist and secretary role. Over the months, we hired people for both of these positions. As I got to know the consultant better, she shared with me that she was tired of traveling around the State as the consultant. I asked if she might like to be the department head at our facility for our new ICF program. She didn't give me an answer, but I went to the superintendent and shared with him our conversation. I suggested that he might want to speak to her about this because what better person to run the program than the person who had been our consultant. The consultant knew all about the mountains of documentation and paperwork that went along with this program. The superintendent offered her the position, and she accepted.

I continued in my regular position. I began to have some more ideas on how we could enhance the students' learning through more gross motor and fine motor play activities. I began discussing these ideas with the head of the physical education program. He also had been thinking along the same lines over the many years he had been employed at NYSSB. He had implemented a couple of his ideas already. We discussed a playground that could be located behind the school. We started talking to other staff members who agreed with the concept. It just so happened my school district had just built a playground that was designed by a playground architect. I informed the superintendent about what we had been talking about and asked if he would approve continuing to explore the possibilities. We continued to meet with staff from all departments getting ideas from them about what they could visualize what could be in this playground. The ideas that came forward took it out of the realm of a playground and put it in the concept of a park. We began to think of it in terms of a sensory park. With the superintendent's approval, we contacted the playground architect to discuss our thoughts. The superintendent also suggested that we meet with our representative from the local Lions Club, as they could partner with us in this undertaking. We met with our local representative, and he was excited about the program. Our local Lions Club had always been most helpful with anything needed for our children. The Lions Club member and our involved group met with the architect to discuss what sensory park would require to make it a reality. He brought up cost considerations, cost of necessary supplies, cost for his services, architectural drawings, his time to meet with the staff for their ideas and input, and supervision of the volunteers while they were constructing the sensory park. It would be necessary to have many, many volunteers to construct a park of this size on a weekend. Food would have to be served to all volunteers on the weekend. Some construction equipment would be needed.

Initial plans began. We set up committees working with Lions Club and their members. Our Lions Club representative and I were appointed cochairpersons. We had a fundraising committee, volunteer committee, committee needed to secure such things as volunteer operators with equipment needed in construction, and committee

Collage of Sensory Park, start to finish

Sensory Park

One activity in Sensory Park

who would be contacting the local stores and such to be volunteering free food and snacks to feed the volunteers during construction weekend. Over the next months, the Lions Club rep, the recreational therapist, and I attended many Lions Club meetings in western New York, to fire up everyone so the students would have a beautiful functional Sensory Park.

I somehow learned of a lawyer who was in control of an estate that was to be used for the blind. He was located in the Ithaca area. I called him, and after describing the sensory park project to him, I asked if he could possibly make a donation from that estate. He was very interested in the park and committed $1,000 to the project. As all the committees continued to work on their projects; several newspapers picked up on the project and decided to write a story about it. The *Batavia Daily News* and the Rochester *Democrat and Chronicle* wrote stories about the project. In the meantime, the superintendent and the business manager of the school were keeping track of donations coming in. After some months, the superintendent and I met to discuss the financial status of the project. He believed that we did not have enough money committed to complete the whole project and wanted to discuss how we could cut the project down. I was shocked and said, "Give me a few minutes. I'll be back." I walked to my office and got the phone number of the lawyer who had already donated $1,000. I returned to the superintendent's office and told him, "I would like to call the lawyer and talk to him about the problem." He agreed, so I made the call in his office. I explained the problem to the lawyer, and he said he was sure he could help. The superintendent and I set a date where we would go to meet him in his office. Several weeks later, we made the trip there with some of the financial figures that we had. The lawyer was very welcoming; when got there, he sat down with us, reviewing the architectural drawings, monies that were being donated, the committees and their work, the publicity that had been received, etc. We were surprised with his answer. He told us that the estate would provide any amount of money that was needed to complete the project but if it took a lot more money from the estate he wanted us to name the park after the person whose estate was being used. We explained to him that the Lions Clubs were very involved in the project and thought that we might name it the Lions Sensory Park. We ended up agreeing that if we had to use a large amount of the money from the estate, we would name it after the person whose estate it was. We left the meeting with a very positive feeling. We knew we wouldn't have to make cuts to the proposed program.

After about five or six months, things were pretty much going the right way, the committees being successful in their endeavors, meetings with the staff and the architect continued, more donations for the project were coming in, and volunteer commitments were overwhelming. We learned that some of the Lions volunteers from, across the State, were actually bringing their motor vehicles and planning to sleep on the school grounds, which had been approved. Others had rooms at the local motels.

About two weeks before the big weekend, the volunteer construction people laid all the sidewalks leading up to where the sensory park would begin. We wanted to be sure all the concrete was cured and dry. The week before, the food committee was getting organized and picking up all the food that was necessary to feed the masses. The excitement for all involved continued to grow. Friday night, the volunteers started showing up. Saturday morning, the architect and volunteers arrived about seven in the morning. Shortly after that, we had a big surprise. A very large truck with markings on the truck, Stanley's Tools, arrived. The driver explained that they had heard about our project and were donating as many tools as needed for people who were working but did not bring tools. All the construction tools that we needed were ours, hammers, saws, etc. What a blessing.

Our architect began assigning a leader for each of the projects and setting up teams for each of the leaders. The leaders all had some background in construction. Our architect had plans drawn up for each team to follow. The park began to evolve. Sensory park was divided into nine major play areas: an obstacle course, a maze, a climbing and stair area, a vehicle area, a rubber band and punching bag room, a swing set, a miniature golf course, a pond for water play, and a garden and green fields. Each area was designed with a separate set of goals and functions in mind. Every area links up to adjacent areas through paths and ramps. There was a wading pool, a ball environment for the kids to waddle around in, and wooden vehicles, a car, fire truck, and a train, which made all kinds of appropriate noises. To cause effect, the children push something, turn a wheel, etc., and they get a response. There was a miniature golf course included, with lights and bells over the holes. There were steps leading up to platforms and slides going down from them, padded tunnels to crawl through, balance beams with guardrails to prevent falls, a rubber bridge, electronics throughout the whole park, etc. These examples give you just a small sampling of what the park was all about. It was designed to allow learning through play and to enhance the children's senses. Sunday night, as the construction came to a close, the park was almost completed, except for a few finishing touches. The children were returning from their homes and finishing up supper. The architect and several of us stood at the top of one of the towers and observed the children walking to the park. The staff took the students on a tour of the park. They were in awe of all the fun things that they would be doing. The playground was also mostly handicapped accessible, as we had children in wheelchairs. The architects said to me, "You were right. This is not a playground. It is truly a park." It was estimated that there were over 1,500 volunteers that participated in this project.

In 1991, sensory park was featured in a book, *Getting in Touch with Play, Creating Environments for Children with Visual Impairments*. Also a poem was written by one of the Spencerport Lions Club members titled *A Dream, a Vision, a Reality, a Sensory Park*. I'm including this poem here in a separate page, along with some sketches, to describe the project. As it turned out, we did not have to use a lot of money from the person's estate, as we continued to get in many more donations.

My time at NYSSB would be over in 1993, as I was retiring. Other things were happening both at NYSSB and at home.

My youngest son was a junior in high school, and he made friends with a foreign exchange student from Denmark, Peter, who sometimes had supper with us. After he had been with his host family for about a month, the son of the host family became terminally ill. Peter notified his parents and his coordinator about the situation. She asked him if there was a family that he might like to stay with. He told her that he would like to stay with the Condidorios. I received a call from his coordinator who described the situation to us and asked if we would consider having Peter live with us for the remainder of the school year. I told her I would discuss it with my family and get back to her. That night, we had a family discussion about this, and they all agreed that they would love to have Peter stay with us. I called this coordinator back and gave her the information. She proceeded to notify Peter's family and the host family, and Peter became our foreign exchange student. He fit in well with our family. He was very respectful and a joy to have around. The kind of Christmas we had was kind of new to him, as his family always went on ski vacations for Christmas. Some of us decided to go Christmas shopping, and he said he would come along. He determined it was a big mistake. He couldn't understand how we could be shopping for three hours, going in stores and sometimes coming out with nothing that we bought. He was glad when we returned home. He loved the rest of the family Christmas festivities. In May, his parents decided to come and visit us. As some of our older children had already left home, we had plenty of room for them. Joe and I were still working at this time, so they spent their time sightseeing in the area. They spent quite a bit of time in Niagara Falls. Most evenings, they ate with us and spent time getting to know one another. One night, they took us and the family out to supper at the Red Osier. At that time, my sister and her husband were also visiting us from Cleveland, and of course, they came to supper with us. We all had a wonderful time. They shared with us that their twenty-fifth wedding anniversary was coming up upcoming in the next few years and their custom was to have a very big celebration for this event. They indicated they would love to have us attend and they would be sending us invitations at the right time. Joe and I and my sister and her husband told them we thought it would be fun if we could make it. Peter's parents left the next day. Peter finished out the semester in June and left for his home. It was sad for all of us, but we knew that this was part of life. Peter surprised us the next Christmas and decided he wanted to come and spend Christmas with us because he liked our celebration.

Chapter 9

As my career as dean of students at the New York State School for the Blind was winding down, these are some memories involving the NYSSB and also of family.

As we were preparing for the summer program one year, the administration requested that I interview and hire the staff, both education aides and residential child care aides, to take the place of those regular staff who chose not to work summer school. The total of both regular and new hires would amount to about thirty-three. This was completed before summer school started. Summer school staff orientation occurs the day before the children start summer school. As I arrived for the orientation day, the superintendent asked me to come to his office. He and the principal informed me that they had asked me to hire three too many new staff. They also informed me that I would have to decide and notify three people who were going to be told that they did not have a summer job. I was angry, to say the least. As I walked out of the office, I threw up my hands and prayed to the Sacred Heart, "I can't deal with this. You need to."

I was moving into the switchboard area, which was just outside the superintendent's office and also connected to the secretary's area, when the phone rang, and the secretary said, "Flo, it's for you."

I answered the phone, and lo and behold, it was one of the new staff members who had had an accident and was unable to come to work. I told her not to worry that we were all set for the summer. Thank you, God, now I only have two to tell. As I walked toward the door, the phone rang again, and it was for me. A regular staff member who usually works summer school told me she could not work that summer due to a family issue. I assured her it was okay and that we would be okay staff-wise. I again said, "Thank You, Jesus. Now I only have to tell one person they don't have a job." Again I started to walk out the door, the phone rang again, and it was for me. Another new hire was calling in to tell me that she could not work this summer as she had planned. I don't remember the reason, but I assured her it was okay. I knew what had just occurred was the most obvious miracle of my life. I knew over my lifetime that many miracles had occurred, but they were not this obvious. The secretary and I just looked at each other and shook our heads in disbelief. What a wonderful way to start this summer school program.

About halfway down my employment at NYSSB, I began taking some courses in counseling, as I found I was doing a lot of counseling with students, staff, and parents. My goal was to get a master's degree in counseling. Albany decided at that time that all education staff, in NYS, who were in supervisory positions needed to get a master's in education to continue in their positions. I changed my major to a master's in education. Fortunately, the courses that I had taken in counseling were able to be used as part of that degree program. In 1982, I received the certification of masters of science in education. Several years later,

State education department then wanted supervisory staff to get another certification. A few years later, I was granted administrator-supervisor certificate for the State of New York.

Also over these years, I took a course in orientation and mobility from Syracuse University. This course taught how the blind used a cane for travel. We had to learn how to use a cane with blindfolds on. To pass this course, we were required to cross Main Street in Batavia, at a red light, with a blindfold on, using a cane. Also we had to go to a restaurant, using a cane and a blindfold on, and order our meal. It had to be something you could cut with a knife and eat, and we also had to pay for our order. There were five of us in the class, and all ended up with food either in our laps or on the floor. During this course, we also went into the shop area at the school, where they had table saws and other equipment. We each took turns putting a piece of wood through the saw on the table. They did have a guard around the table saw, but we were all a little leery of getting cut when we were using the saw. We all passed the course. The credit we gained went toward our master's program. We also learned to read braille, no credit, but good experience. The residential and educational staff had to take a course in sign language, as we had a number of students who were deaf-blind and used sign language for communication.

Over these and the next few years, I had many health issues. I had back surgery, neck surgery, stomach surgery, gallbladder surgery complicated by pancreatitis, and a right hip replacement. I also had a severe allergic reaction to an

Beth's wedding

antibiotic. The doctor had to intubate me, and I was put in an induced coma for about ten days. It was a harrowing experience for my family. Joe, while extending a ladder, experienced a rotor cuff tear and required surgery. We managed to survive all these incidences.

Our youngest daughter was planning on getting married in November of 1985, her fiancé was in the Marines. She came home on a Wednesday in September of that year and informed us that they were going to have to get married the coming weekend as her fiancé wasn't sure he could get the time off in November. She explained that they would just get married at the justice of peace. I told her no, as we had planned a wedding for her and the wedding would take place on that weekend. We contacted the party house, which was owned by a friend of ours and asked if they had anything available on the weekend. Fortunately, Sunday was available, and they had food in the freezer to be able to put on the dinner. We quickly called all the relatives and invited them to the wedding, letting them know that we would contact them later about the details. We contacted a priest, who had been a teacher for her at Notre Dame, and he was free to perform the ceremony Sunday, and he set it up at Saint Anthony's Church in Batavia. The priest did insist on meeting with my daughter and her fiancé to go over the meaning of marriage. They did willingly meet with the priest. We were able to secure a florist, who had the flower bouquets made for the wedding, a photographer to take pictures, and a small band to play at the wedding. My daughter wore her sister-in-law's wedding gown and veil, which fit her to a tee. My older daughter flew in from Texas to be her maid of honor, borrowing a bridesmaid dress, to wear, from another sister-in-law. The wedding went off like clockwork, much to our surprise, just another example of Jesus being with us all the way.

During these years, we liked to take one day a year and make Saint Joseph bread in honor of Saint Joseph. Whatever women and grandchildren were around came over to the house, along with some neighborhood kids. The adults prepared the dough and let it rise. The children then took over, with the help of the women, forming it into shapes. Braided breads represented the Blessed Mother, beards and staffs for St. Joseph, eyes for Saint Lucy, and baby forms for Jesus. Breads were then brushed with egg white and baked.

All had bread loaves to take home with them. Other loaves were given to friends and neighbors.

Joe retired in 1991, as Kodak offered their employees a package that he could not refuse. Not only would his pension kick in, but he would be getting what they called a bridge to Social Security. Each month, they would be giving him additional money, equivalent to what his Social Security would be, until he reached sixty-two. At this time, he was fifty-six. After he retired, he took over all the household duties, including cooking supper. I retired two years later when I was fifty-nine, as I now had my twenty years in and could receive my pension.

Shortly after retirement, we received an invitation to Peter's parents twenty-fifth wedding anniversary party. My sister and her husband and Joe and I attended their party in Denmark. I was terrified of flying but survived the trip. We stayed at the corporate apartment, which was owned by the parents. They were wonderful hosts. As they had a very large sailing boat, one day, we sailed across the water to Sweden and had lunch. It was an awesome experience. Customs there for a twenty-fifth-year celebration started with a band going to their home and waking them up. We had breakfast with them, and then came the big festivities. About four in the afternoon, we drove to the edge of the park, where the festivities were going to take place. We were met with a horse and carriage driven by a man with a tall hat and transported to a castle-like restaurant. The place was beautiful, the dinner was delicious, and the dancing to a live band afterward was wonderful. All the people at the party made us feel so welcome.

The next day, all the guys went to see a big soccer game. My sister and I decided to go exploring a little bit. Outside our building were what they called walking streets. We walked up and down them for hours. As we became tired, my sister said, "Let's get a cab."

I looked at her and said, "Where are we going to tell him to take us?" Neither of us knew the address of where we were staying. We were lost. I said to her, "We will stop some of the young people because I know they all take English in school. We can explain our situation to them and ask for help." We did remember that we lived close to one of the castles, so we thought that might help.

We stopped some of the older students and explained our situation. We asked if they could help us, and immediately they were willing. After describing what we thought we were staying and the information about the castle, they said they knew where we were going. We walked for quite a while and found a castle, but it was the wrong castle. When we told them it was the wrong castle, they thought for a minute and said, "Oh, now we know what castle you mean." So we started out walking again, and pretty soon, we did see the right castle. We thanked them and told them that we could now get to our apartment because now we knew the way. I'm sure that over the years, they have shared this funny story with their friends about the lost American ladies. When our husbands returned, they didn't think the story was so funny.

Since Germany was so close, we thought we would take a day trip to see different parts of Germany. It was very interesting to see the difference between the development of East Germany and West Germany since the war. We prepared to return home after about a week. It was sad to say goodbye to our Peter and his parents, who had been such wonderful hosts. We shared our stories with our families when we returned home.

My sister and her husband owned a condo in Naples, Florida. They invited us to visit them for the winter. We did stay with them during the winter months the next year. They wintered with a group of friends of theirs from their home area every winter. We became part of that group, renting every winter in Naples for the next twelve years. Every Sunday during this time, we would play cards. The couples would take turns hosting the party card games. The host each Sunday would prepare the meal. One time when it was our turn to host, I made apple pies for dessert. I no longer made the crust from scratch but used Pillsbury pie crust. One of the men complimented me, saying that that was the best pie crust he had ever tasted. Us women all laughed at that and forever became Pillsbury pie crust fans. Over those twelve years, we would go out boating, fishing, dancing, and having all kinds of fun.

The months we were home, we continued to have our card games, canasta, every week with the same three couples. Of course, the same rules applied. Whatever couple was hosting cooked the meal, men against the women, and whoever lost had to clean up the kitchen and do the dishes. By then, we had been playing cards over fifty years off and on.

Over the years, as the children moved out, we had an open-door policy. Children could come home and stay there if they needed a place until the issues they were dealing got resolved. Our son who was a contractor and built several new homes for his family stayed with us after his former home was sold but his new home was not complete yet. A daughter and children whose husband was in service stayed for a time until he was relocated. Our other daughter and son stayed for a time when she returned from California. It was fun having these families with their little children staying with us. These episodes gave us a chance to get to know our little grandchildren better. As we had only our youngest child living at home, we decided to sell our home and rent an apartment. After selling our home, we found a two-story apartment in Batavia; it was new and had three bedrooms. We were not happy in Batavia, as our family and friends were in LeRoy. We moved back to LeRoy after a year, and we rented a two-story, two-bedroom home. After about a year, we realized that I was having a lot of difficulty going up and down the stairs. We decided to build a three-bedroom ranch home that was handicapped accessible, as I was experiencing more health problems from the post-polio syndrome. As we began building, one of our sons, who was returning from California after many years away, decided he was going to relocate back to LeRoy. He asked if we could build a bedroom in the basement for him. We agreed to this. Another son, as he learned about this, asked if we could also build him a bedroom in the basement. He had been selling meat door to door all over western New York and living in motel rooms. We agreed and had our builder, who was another son, add two bedrooms and a full bath in the basement. By this time, our youngest son was out of the house and married.

We moved into our new home. We continued with our card playing and spaghetti Sunday dinners. One of our granddaughters who was in college was required to write a poem about a tradition in their family. She chose to write about our spaghetti Sunday dinners.

"Sundays"

Sunday afternoons are special to me,
Grandma and Grandpa's is where I'll be.
The house is full, the house is loud.
Almost 50 people make up the crowd.
Aunts are there and uncles and cousins.
People keep arriving by the dozens.
The smells are wafting through the air,
There is barely room for every chair.
"Short or Long?" my grandpa asks.
All the women take on different tasks.
Bread and sauce and salad too.
The crazy house resembles a zoo.
We eat and eat until we can't eat anymore.
Usually there is food all over the floor.
The messy kids wash up at the sink.
They are off to play before you can blink.
The ladies start to clean the dishes and plates,
while the TV is taken over by their mates.
Laughter is heard from the children at play.
And anyone who asks about dessert is shooed away.

Once the kitchen is clear and dessert is brought out.
No matter how full you are, you can't go without.
We say our goodbyes and "See you next week."
I love my family because we are unique.

I included this poem because it gives you the essence of what this family is all about.

When my youngest daughter's husband was no longer in service, they came back to Le Roy to live. They built a house right next door to where we lived. Shortly after, my oldest daughter bought a house right around the corner from us. It was a delight to have them both so close. Several of the boys also bought or built new homes in Le Roy. Some of the homes were large enough, so we no longer had to host Christmas or the other holidays. Also, one of our sons has a very large swimming pool at his house and hosted summer activities.

Chapter 10

The next years, at our new home, things were not as eventful. Of course, some people would consider this not to be true. We continued to have the noisy Sundays, the card games, visitations from all our family and friends, trips to Florida each year, etc. We became used to our slowed-down lifestyle, and we now had time for things like reading, extra prayers, Facebook, communicating by phone to people that lived farther away, etc.

About ten or fifteen years ago, as some of the residential staff and the education staff that I supervised began to retire, each group began having their own gatherings. I was honored to be included in each of these groups. It's been a pleasure to share all the things we have been doing now and learning about the growth of their families. Reminiscing about the past experiences at the New York State School for the Blind has been a lot of fun.

I was selected as the Outstanding Italian-American Woman in 2016 by the Paolo Busty Cultural Foundation. This was considered to be quite an honor. I received several congratulatory letters from New York State representatives. This foundation is countywide. Both the chosen man and the woman who received this award were honored at a fundraising dinner. The local paper ran quite a large article on it.

In 2016, Joe was inducted into the Sports Hall of Fame in our local school district. He played all four sports in all his high school years. He excelled in football and was cocaptain of his team in his senior year. The few inductees were honored at a large dinner that year.

After living in our new home for about fifteen years, I was experiencing even more problems walking and having a lot of back pain. We consulted with a spine doctor who, after doing more testing and more X-rays, determined that I would have to be in electric wheelchair. My spine had a serious curvature and was completely fused. I could no longer depend on my legs. I was shocked at first and upset. The doctor wrote a script to Medicare with all the medical jargon necessary for them to purchase the chair. We went to the store, got approved by Medicare, and picked out an electric wheelchair. The process took over a month. They finally delivered my electric wheelchair to my home. The next problem we faced was how we would transport this wheelchair. We pulled up eBay on the computer and looked for a vehicle that had a lift for an electric wheelchair in it. The one that looked the most appropriate was located in Western Pennsylvania. I phoned them and asked if they could send us pictures of the vehicle. They agreed, but they also said that they had promised the vehicle to someone else in their neighborhood, who had a month to either take it or they would put it back on the market. We were disappointed but held out hope. Over the next month, we looked at other vehicles, but they were not what we were looking for. The month passed, and we made another call to them. They informed us that the other people decided not to take it and that if we wanted it we could have it. Joe and one of our sons took a ride down to purchase the vehicle, if it fit our needs. The van was in great shape with a heavy-duty lift. Since the man's wife could no longer use the electric wheelchair in the vehicle, he offered to throw this in with this deal. This was wonderful, as now we would not have to bring the wheelchair that we used inside, out to the car. We now had one to use inside and one to use outside. The couple who owned the van was very cordial and wanted to do everything to help. They took them where they could get a temporary license plate and even provided lunch for them.

As I began using the wheelchairs continually, I realized how it had freed me up to do everything I wanted to do. I could now attend grandchildren's sports activities, inside and outside. I could go to lunch with friends, easily attend mass, and even go to playgrounds with my grandchildren. I knew Jesus was once again looking after us. Joe and I watched a movie on TV called *God Winks*. It was about a woman in the movie who believed that coincidences in our lives were actually God's winks. I love the concept. So many people in my life would say to one another what a coincidence.

After twenty-two years in our beautiful ranch home, we felt that we needed to make a change. I was having more trouble with my health, and Joe had new health issues. I had been in an electric wheelchair for five years due to my deteriorating spine. We informed all our children about our intention. I asked Joe if we could go look at an independent living program in Le Roy. He agreed, and we came to tour St. Anne's The Greens. We were very impressed. We knew if we were accepted and came to this facility we would require a two-bedroom, two-bath apartment. It was considered a double unit. None of the nine double units were available at this time. We would have to wait for one to become available. The two boys who were living with us knew they had to get their own apartments. They began applying for apartments in the area.

Our children were all supportive of the move as they knew it was getting difficult for their father and me to maintain and do the upkeep of our home even with the help of our sons who lived with us. Much to our surprise, a unit that we were looking for became available two months later. We put our house on the market, and in one day, it was sold. It took almost three months to finalize the sale. We moved into The Greens on August 1, 2022. Our sons also found their one-bedroom apartments to rent and successfully moved in and are all settled.

During the last years in our house, we did experience some sadness in our lives. One of our beautiful daughters-in-law passed away from cancer. She left a loving husband and three very sad adult children. One of our granddaughters also passed away, leaving two beautiful two-year-old twin girls. They reside with their father. Their maternal grandparents are very involved with their upbringing. Their older twin cousins, from the time that the little twins were two, have been involved in their care. The two sets of twin girls have developed a close bond. Over the years, we have had the two sets of twins and their father for supper one day a week, for many weeks. This allowed us to get to know both sets of twins even better. Also it gave the father a break by not having to prepare supper for them one night a week.

Many people over the years have said to us, "You have the perfect family. How did you do it?" I assured them that no one has a perfect family and all families have problems. Siblings have conflicts, which sometimes are difficult to resolve. Parents and their children have issues. We brought our children up to be free thinkers. They each have their own beliefs in religion, politics, family issues, etc. As parents, we encourage them to be more forgiving, more accepting, and less discriminating against those who think differently than them.

We have now been living at The Greens for about six months. We love it here. We knew many of the people who live here as some were classmates of my husband's, some were former neighbors, and some people's children, who grew up with our children. We, as parents, participated with them in Boy Scouts, Little League, football leagues, church, etc. Several residents used to bring their children to my day care center. We also now have become friends with many of the other residents here who we did not know before.

What is there not to like here, when someone comes to clean your house and change your sheets and launders all your sheets and towels. The cooks prepare your breakfast and supper. We get a menu weekly and have a choice of three entrees for supper plus a salad, soup, and dessert. We go into the dining room, which is set up like restaurant style, four to a table. We are waited on by the dining staff but don't have to leave a tip. All the staff from the administration down are cordial and will help you whenever you need it. If you have a problem, your meals can be brought to your room. Each month, you are given a calendar with all the activities listed on it. There are games set up, like bingo, etc., exercise programs, musical entertainment, social times, special meetings, etc. Also if you need a ride to a medical appointment, transportation is provided. They do all the upkeep on the outside like snow removal, lawn mowing, and trimming of the bushes.

If there is a maintenance issue inside the apartment, all you have to do is call the desk, and they have someone come and take care of it. At this point in our lives, Joe and I are eighty-eight and eighty-nine. This year, we will celebrate seventy years of marriage on Thanksgiving weekend. We have ten children, twenty-three grandchildren, and nineteen great-grandchildren, and two of our granddaughters are expecting a new baby. We are very blessed and happy with our lives.

Family Wedding

A Dream, a Vision, a Reality, a Sensory Park

It started with a caring thought
and soon became a spark
that ignited the big effort
to build our kids a park.

They had a park once before
but this was not to be the same
and looking back it's evident
this puts that one to shame.

And so the plans were started
with meetings to discuss
the how's, the why's, the where, and the when
and rant and rave and fuss.

Bob Leathers was invited
to offer his special design
of mazes, slides and fun, kid things
but suited to the blind.

FLORENCE CONDIDORIO

As plans progressed and things took shape
we realized quite fast
that a lot of details must be satisfied
and an army was needed for this task.

As the date drew near, the last days of May
Bob Leathers was often heard to say, without the required volunteers on hand
we'll have to scale back our plans.

Flo forged ahead with determination
and Barb worked long and hard;
before too long things started appearing
out in the maintenance yard.

The sidewalks were the first part
and we worked hard and long;
with all the measuring and checking
we got one in that's wrong.

The posts were next
or the post holes I should say,
with the junk that was buried
that went every which way.

HOW WE GROW

But soon there arose as if in a dream
a magical city of timbers and beams
with spires and towers that rise to the sky
while the sun shone so hot, you thought you would die.

Each volunteer fitted pieces precise
they wanted it all to be finished so nice
and no task was refused by the masses of folks,
from carrying racks to supplying the cokes.

Ah, we stopped twice a day to fill up our tanks
the people who served us deserve all our thanks
while the food that was dominated every last thing
was simply delicious and fit for a king.

At times it seemed we would make it
as volunteers showed up by galore
and as supplies diminish
Art Roth went to the store.

With Sunday well upon us
we knew we would miss our mark
so we didn't get it all quite done
but we opened Sensory Park

FLORENCE CONDIDORIO

Well the kids came in and went around
to try the different things
you know from their giggles, laughs, and smiles
that the effort you made were all worthwhile.

For all the people be they big or just small
they answered the need, no task was too tall,
we started out strangers but in the end
we hugged and embraced and wound up as good friends.

By Ed Nau
Spencerport Lions Club

About the Author

Florence Condidorio is an eighty-nine-year-old woman, and she and her husband will celebrate seventy years of marriage in November of this year. They are parents to ten children and grandparents to twenty-three grandchildren and nineteen great-grandchildren. She ran a state-operated day care center in her home for many years. After their ninth child was born, she attended college and, after four years, was awarded a bachelor's degree in education for elementary children. She was contacted by the New York State School for the Blind and asked to interview for a position as dean of students at their facility. She was employed there for twenty years.

Printed in the USA
CPSIA information can be obtained
at www.ICGtesting.com
LVHW020745051023
760085LV00053B/1094